MOVING & LEARNING

with Your Child

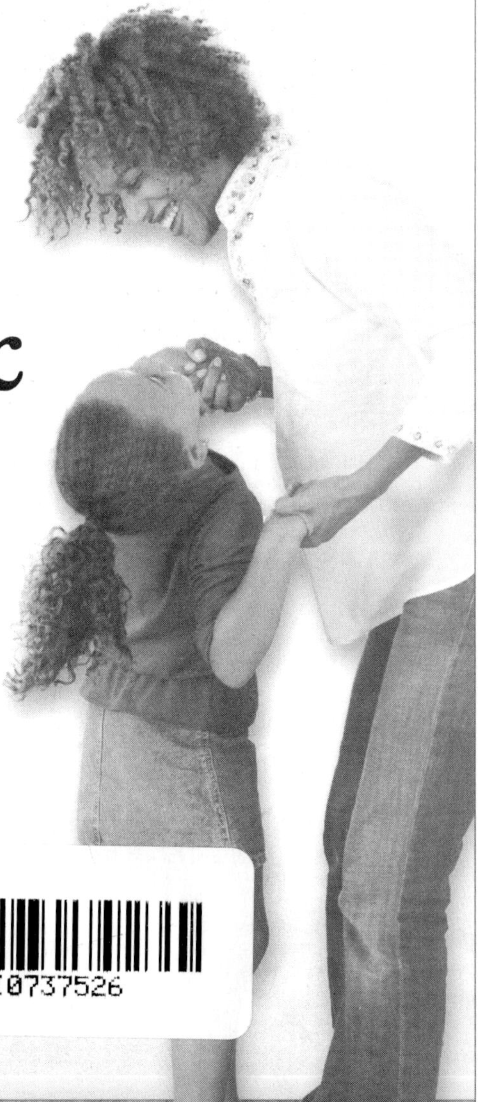

RAE PICA

MOVING AND LEARNING WITH YOUR CHILD

Your child's physical, social/emotional, and cognitive development overlap—children do not differentiate among thinking, feeling, and moving. Thus, when your child learns something related to one area, it impacts the others! The purpose of this booklet is to help you understand movement's role in the physical, social/emotional, and cognitive development of your child. We'll look at

- the health benefits of physical activity,
- how moving and playing together helps children learn to get along and become part of a society,
- how physical activity can help make your child "smarter,"
- how the mind and body are linked, and
- what you can do at home to contribute to all of these benefits.

Since movement is most often associated with physical results, let's start there.

PHYSICAL DEVELOPMENT

Perhaps the simplest and most important reason children should be allowed and encouraged to move is to develop movement skills.

As children grow, they need support to develop their physical skills, which don't automatically mature on their own. (You've heard the expression, "She throws like a girl"—or, even more insulting, "He throws like a girl." In either case, they're talking about a child who throws at an immature level.)

Achieving a mature level for the performance of motor skills may not seem like a big deal, considering not every child will want to go on to become an athlete or a dancer. But it *is* a big deal when we consider that children who feel confident in their movement skills are the ones who are likely to continue moving throughout their lives. Adolescents and adults who haven't acquired and mastered fundamental movement skills are the ones who shy away from physical activity because the movements required feel unnatural and overly strenuous. Also, the fear of failing and looking foolish is a powerful deterrent.

Of course, the other important reason why children should be allowed and encouraged to move is because of the serious health risks associated with lack of physical activity. Among them are heart disease risk factors such as hypertension, obesity, and arteriosclerosis, as well as type 2 diabetes.

Conversely, regular physical activity

- helps build and maintain healthy bones, muscles, and joints;
- increases the body's infection-fighting white blood cells and germ-fighting antibodies;

- helps control weight;
- reduces the risk of dying from heart disease;
- reduces the risk of developing diabetes; and
- stimulates growth of the heart, lungs, and other vital organs in children.

What You Can Do at Home

Today's young children expend far less energy in physical activity than did their predecessors. It's unlikely your child is participating in the 60 minutes a day of structured physical activity (as in physical education or a family game of tag, for example) plus 60 minutes a day of unstructured physical activity (free play) recommended by SHAPE America, the organization of health and physical educators, the Institute of Medicine, and other health organizations.

Here are some activities to help ensure that your child practices and refines his motor skills and achieves the health benefits of physical activity:

> **In and Around.** Set up an obstacle course using large empty boxes to move through, chairs or other pieces of furniture big enough to move under, jump ropes to move over, or small items to move around. Then lead your child through the maze. Every time you play this game, arrange the objects differently and even give them different purposes. For instance, if the jump rope was originally lying on the floor for leaping or jumping over, you can later suspend it between two pieces of furniture for creeping under.

Chasing Bubbles. Want to give your child a reason to run and jump? Take her outside and invite her to catch the bubbles you blow.

Follow the Leader. Lead the way around the living room or backyard, performing as many different locomotor (traveling) skills as you know your child can replicate. Give your child a turn at being the leader.

Traffic Lights. Gather three large pieces of paper—one red, one green, and one yellow. When you hold up the green paper, have your child walk. When you hold up the yellow, he or she should walk in place. For red, your child should stop and wait. Start with walking until your child gets the hang of the game. Then play using other locomotor skills.

And don't forget such simple things as taking a family walk after dinner, planning outings that involve physical activity rather than sedentary behaviors, and buying movement-oriented toys, like balls in a variety of shapes, sizes, and textures; roller skates; a jump rope; juggling scarves; or a little red wagon.

Perhaps most importantly, provide plenty of time for your child to play outside. That's where children expend the most energy and have the space necessary to practice gross motor skills.

SOCIAL/EMOTIONAL DEVELOPMENT

Movement's role in your child's social/emotional development may be a bit challenging to envision, but physical activity and play have much to do with how your child will grow socially and emotionally. Here's just some of what the research tells us:

- Physical activity is consistently associated with higher levels of self-esteem (the value a child places on herself) and self-concept (the understanding the child has of herself).
- Because they offer young children independence, muscle control and good eye-hand coordination enhance children's feelings of effectiveness.
- Physical activity contributes to better body image and mood and to an overall improved sense of well-being.
- Physical activity can have a positive impact on moral reasoning.
- Physically skilled children tend to be more popular with their peers, even among preschoolers.

When children participate in self-selected, self-directed physical activity, their social/emotional skills increase. By organizing their own games and negotiating rules, they begin to acquire flexibility in their thinking, develop problem-solving skills, learn conflict resolution, and take the perspective of others (an absolutely vital social skill).

Child-organized games also allow participants to practice leadership skills and self-discipline. This lends itself to positive self-esteem, which some contend is necessary for the development of trust in human relationships. Children engaged in self-directed physical activity gain a sense of autonomy (self-sufficiency) and learn to share, take turns, and develop impulse control. They're not afraid to take creative risks or to make a mistake because, in true play (as opposed to organized sports), there's no such thing as failure. Mistakes made are simply corrected. Although a child may not always get his way, this, too, teaches an important lesson.

When children cooperate with one another in physical activity, as opposed to competing against each other, each child realizes he or she plays a vital role in the outcome, and each accepts the responsibility of fulfilling that role. They also learn to become tolerant of others' ideas and to accept the similarities and differences of others. And cooperative activities seldom cause the feelings of inferiority that can result from the comparisons made during competition. On the contrary, because cooperative and noncompetitive activities lead to a greater chance for success, they generate greater confidence in children.

What You Can Do at Home

Focus on the *joy* of physical activity and play! For young children, the importance of *process* far surpasses that of *product*. In physical activities, the process is in the playing. Children don't care about winning or about how well they're playing—unless the important adults in their lives make it clear that *they* care about such things. What's important to children is that they have fun!

Here are some simple cooperative games that offer many social/emotional, as well as cognitive and physical, benefits. These partner activities are for you and your child or for children to play together.

Mirror Game. Partners stand facing each other. One partner performs a series of simple movements that the second partner mirrors. The object is not to try to trick each other but to resemble a mirror reflection as closely as possible.

Balance, Balance. Partners stand with their hands on one another's shoulders, or holding hands. They must then maintain a steady balance while trying to: stand on only one foot each; leaning forward, backward, to one side, and to the other side; rising onto tiptoes; rising onto tiptoes and leaning in different directions.

It Takes Two. This activity requires partners to connect various body parts (matching parts, like right hands, left elbows, or right feet; or nonmatching parts, like a hand and an elbow, or an elbow and a shoulder. There are two objects to the game: to stay connected and to see how many ways it's possible to move while remaining connected.

Footsie Rolls. This is a challenging game that requires some space but is a lot of fun. Partners lie on their backs with the soles of their feet together. Then they must see how far they can roll without their feet breaking contact!

Provide your child with plenty of time and opportunity to play with other children, without adult direction or rules. She or he will gain self-sufficiency and positive self-esteem from these experiences as well as important social skills that will last a lifetime.

COGNITIVE DEVELOPMENT

What could movement possibly have to do with learning? As it turns out, plenty!

Einstein nicely said that, "Learning is experience. Everything else is just information." Studies of how young children learn have proven that they especially acquire knowledge experientially—through play, experimentation, exploration, and discovery.

Thanks to advances in brain research, we also now know that most of the brain is activated during physical activity—much more so than when doing seat work. In fact, sitting for more than ten minutes at a stretch increases fatigue and reduces concentration! Moderate- to vigorous-intensity movement, on the other hand, feeds oxygen, water, and glucose (brain food) to the brain, optimizing its performance.

All of this, of course, contradicts the long-standing belief that children learn best when they're sitting still and listening or working quietly at their desks. It also helps us understand why children who participate in daily physical education have been shown to perform better academically and to have a better attitude toward school.

What You Can Do at Home

When children move over, under, around, through, beside, and near objects and others, they better grasp the meaning of these concepts. When they perform a "slow walk" or skip "lightly," adjectives and adverbs become much more than abstract ideas. When they're given the opportunity to physically demonstrate such action words as *stomp, pounce, stalk,* or *slither*—or descriptive words such as *smooth, strong, gentle,* or *enormous*—word comprehension is immediate and long-lasting. Similarly, if children move their bodies in high, low, wide, and narrow ways, they'll have a much greater understanding of these quantitative concepts (critical to the language of mathematics)—and opposites—than do children who are merely presented with the words and their definitions.

Here are some fun learning activities to try at home:

Math with Body Parts. Ask your child to place just five body parts, for example, on the floor. Point out—and count—the parts touching the floor. Now ask him to subtract one body part. How many are now touching the floor? Ask him to add one body part but to make it a different part than the one he removed. Continue in this manner, offering your child the opportunity to experience counting and simple computation.

House Painting. Give your child a paintbrush and a bucket of water and let her "paint" the outside of the house. She'll get some much-needed upper-torso exercise while simultaneously learning lessons about absorption and evaporation.

Skywriting. Show your child some letters or numbers. Then invite him to "write" each, one at a time, in the air in front of him, first with a finger on his dominant hand,

and then with other body parts: elbow, a knee, the top of the head, the nose, or his belly button!

Active Listening. The next time you read a story to your child, invite her to act it out while listening! She'll absorb and retain much more of the story by using multiple senses.

It's no wonder research shows that movement is the young child's preferred mode of learning—because children best *comprehend* concepts that are experienced physically.

This is a family companion published by Redleaf Press on the importance of movement in early childhood. This family companion supports the Moving & Learning series by Rae Pica and *One, Two, What Can I Do?* and *Dance, Turn, Hop, Learn* by Connie Bergstein Dow.

Published by Redleaf Press
10 Yorkton Court
St. Paul, MN 55117
www.redleafpress.org

Cover design by Douglas Schmitz
Cover photograph © ThinkStock/Jupiterimages
Illustrations by Chris Wold Dyrud
Printed in the United States of America

ISBN 978-1-60554-413-7

Redleaf Press®
www.redleafpress.org
800-423-8309